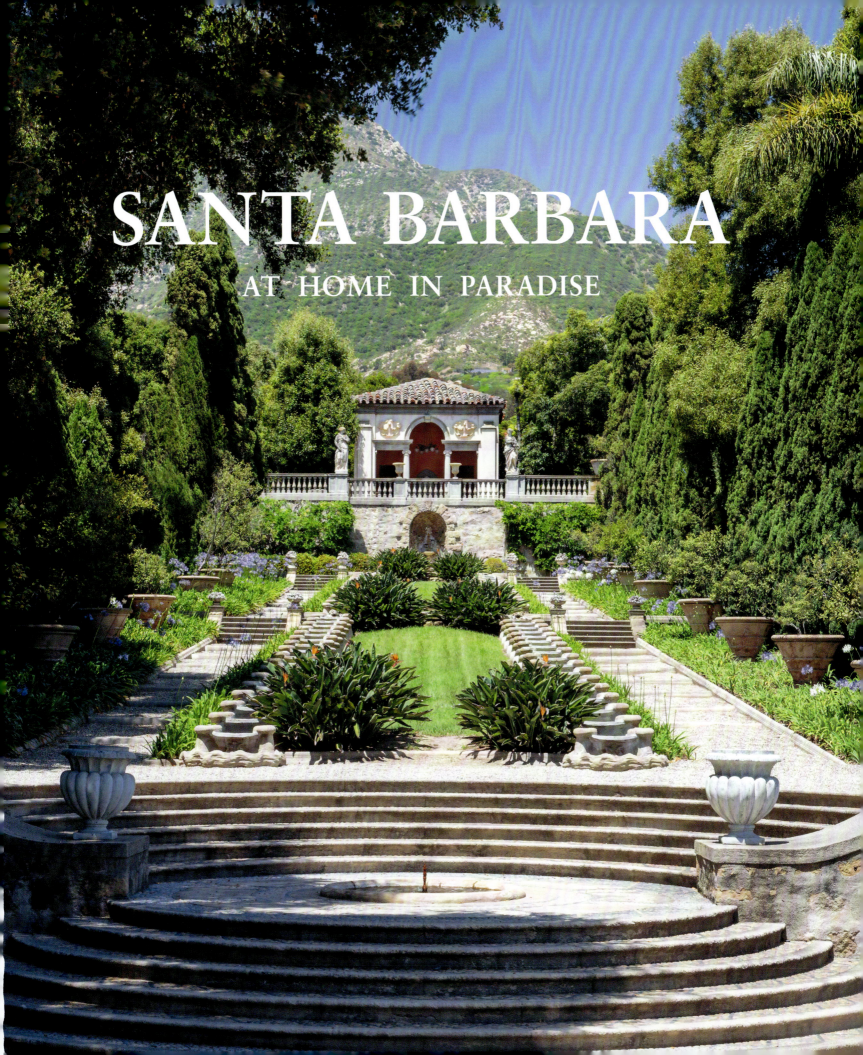

SANTA BARBARA
AT HOME IN PARADISE

SANTA BARBARA

AT HOME IN PARADISE

Douglas Woods
Photography by Matt Walla

RIZZOLI
NEW YORK
New York · Paris · London · Milan

First published in the United States of America in 2025 by
RIZZOLI INTERNATIONAL PUBLICATIONS, INC.
49 West 27th Street, New York, NY 10001
www.rizzoliusa.com

© 2025 Rizzoli International Publications, Inc.
Text (except as noted below) © 2025 Douglas Woods
Photography © 2025 Matt Walla
Foreword by Marc Appleton
Gardens in Paradise, essay by M. Brian Tichenor

Publisher: Charles Miers
Editor: Douglas Curran
Production Manager: Colin Hough Trapp
Managing Editor: Lynn Scrabis
Copy Editor: Victoria Brown
Proofreader: Sarah Stump
Design Manager: Tim Biddick

Designed by Aldo Sampieri

All rights reserved. No part of this publication may be reproduced, stored in a retrieval system, or transmitted in any form or by any means, electronic, mechanical, photocopying, recording, or otherwise, without prior consent of the publisher.

Printed and bound in China

2025 2026 2027 2028 2029 / 10 9 8 7 6 5 4 3 2 1

ISBN-13: 978-0-8478-4269-8
Library of Congress Control Number: 2024945092

Instagram.com/RizzoliBooks
Facebook.com/RizzoliNewYork
X: @Rizzoli_Books
Youtube.com/user/RizzoliNY

Page 1: The grand fountains at Casa Bienvenida designed by Addison Mizner. The teahouse designed by Mary McLaughlin Craig.

Pages 2-3: Montalba, overlooking the coastline of Summerland to Carpinteria.

Pages 4-5: Casa de Leon, with a view of downtown Santa Barbara and the Channel Islands beyond.

Pages 6-7: The pool house at Villa Corbeau designed by Appleton & Associates.

CONTENTS

Foreword by Marc Appleton	10
California Dreamin', An Introduction	14
THE EARLY DAYS	22
Rancho Santa Clara del Norte, Saticoy, 1837–Today	
Calkins Cottage, Santa Barbara, 1896	
Twin Peaks Ranch, Ojai, 1920–Today	
SPANISH THREADS	54
Plaza Rubio, Santa Barbara, 1925	
MONTEREY COLONIAL	66
Las Jacarandas, Riley House, Montecito, 1928	
McKee House, Montecito, 1926–Today	
GEORGE WASHINGTON SMITH, ARCHITECT	88
Essay by Douglas Woods	
Canby, Cunningham House, Montecito, 1922–1925	
Isham Honeymoon Cottage and Natatorium, Carpinteria, 1920–1928	
SMITH'S CONTINUING INFLUENCE	118
Casa de Leon, Santa Barbara Riviera, 1964–Today	
Casa de Seville, Montecito, 2005	

GARDENS IN PARADISE   140
    Essay by M. Brian Tichenor
    Lotusland, Montecito, 1882–1920

OTHER IDIOMS   156
    Paraíso Imaginado, Santa Barbara, 1995
    Montecito Creole, Montecito, 1971
    Montalba, Summerland, 1995

GREAT ESTATES   196
    Billings Estate, Eucalyptus Hill, 1926
    Bellosguardo, Clark Estate, Santa Barbara, 1936
    Casa Bienvenida, Dieterich Estate, Montecito, 1928–1931
    Arcady Pavilion, Knapp Estate, Montecito, 1905–Today
    Villa Corbeau, Montecito, 2006

Acknowledgments   256

FOREWORD

As advertised by most tour guides and national real estate agents, the Santa Barbara area is indeed a paradise. Those lucky enough to have homes here would agree. What makes it so?

The 840-mile-long coast of California enjoys the prospect of spectacular views of the Pacific Ocean. People assume that the coastline faces west, and most of it does. About a third of the way up as one heads north, however, the coast gradually rotates until at a certain point it is actually facing south rather than west, a subtle shift that is imperceptible to the traveler but one which has significant geophysical consequences. Santa Barbara happens to be at that south-facing point!

This southern orientation towards the ocean combines with an abrupt backdrop of the east to west Santa Ynez Mountains, which rise rapidly from sea level to heights of four- to five-thousand feet. As in the South of France, this orientation and steep backdrop creates a uniquely Mediterranean climate for the area. No wonder, then, that a kind of paradise grew and prospered here.

We were by no means the first to discover this. California's Santa Barbara area was a favored part of the native Chumash people's dominion for thousands of years before it was cavalierly claimed as Spanish territory in the sixteenth century. Spanish occupation accelerated in the eighteenth century, when Spanish Franciscan priests began establishing a chain of missions in an effort to control the land and convert the native population to Catholicism. The Mission Santa Barbara—"Queen of the Missions"—was founded in 1786, the tenth of what would ultimately be twenty-one mission outposts in Alta California.

Spanish control, however, ended in 1821 when Mexican separatists succeeded in taking over the Spanish territories, secularizing the mission properties and granting private sales to promote settlement and agricultural development rather than Christianity. The New Mexican Republic was in turn very short-lived: when the 1846 Mexican-American war was settled by treaty in 1848, Texas, New Mexico, Arizona, Utah, Nevada, Colorado, and California were ceded to an even more greedy and powerful United States. It is thus within only the last century and a half that Santa Barbara has developed its reputation for U.S. citizens as a resort destination and eminently desirable place to live.

There is an assumption that Spanish Colonial Revival is the predominant style which defines Santa Barbara architecture. Here, Douglas Woods pays homage to that heritage and its well-documented local history, focusing in particular on the work and influence of noted local architect George Washington Smith. Yet the selection of unique homes in this book—freshly and engagingly photographed by Matt Walla—captures a longer time frame and a greater diversity of architectural styles, set in landscapes that are unmistakably Southern California.

Happily these selections do not follow a formula of trendy designs. They are surprisingly and refreshingly different than most contemporary examples of fashionable homes. Starting with Rancho Santa Clara del Norte (1837–1900) and ending with Villa Corbeau (2006), they definitely say "home" and suggest domestic paradise, but in quiet, unexpected ways.

Since our firm was involved as architect in the design of a couple of his selections, I vacillated and almost recused myself from agreeing to write this Foreword. But I'm so glad I didn't, because *Santa Barbara: At Home in Paradise* is a wonderful addition to Santa Barbara's story, and its allure will likely enjoy a much longer arc than most.

– Marc Appleton

Opposite: The hallway at the Canby, Cunningham House by George Washington Smith.

Following Pages: Casa Bienvenida's south garden, with eucalyptus.

CALIFORNIA DREAMIN'
An Introduction

The American Riviera. Modern Americans have been referring to this region as such since at least the 1880s, from *Sunset* magazine and tourism pamphlets to cruise ship brochures today. This majestic spot of California coastline incorporating Ventura and Santa Barbara counties is home to a collection of bucolic communities that include Ojai, Carpinteria, Montecito, Summerland, and Santa Barbara—the historic and cultural heart of the region. As the locals like to say, they live in paradise, and they aren't wrong.

The Channel Islands and the Santa Barbara coastland is the oldest documented continuously populated place in North America with a rich, complex, and tragic cultural history. Santa Barbara was so named when explorer Sebastián Vizcaíno sailed the harbor on the saint's feast day while mapping the California coast in 1602; he named the islands in her honor. Vizcaíno was not, however, the first European to become enamored with the region. In 1542 Portuguese navigator Juan Rodríguez Cabrillo, sailing under the Spanish flag, reached these shores and claimed the area in the name of the Spanish Crown. He couldn't be faulted for wanting dominion over what might have been the most beautiful coastal region he had ever seen. Of course, the native Chumash people had already been there for at least ten thousand years or so, and they enjoyed a thriving and peaceful culture, traveling between the coast and islands in redwood *tomol* canoes, the oldest example of ocean-worthy watercraft in North America. Cabrillo said of the Chumash, with whom he stayed for two weeks, in a letter from 1542 that "the natives are of superior caste; expert canoemen, and anglers." He stayed with them for two weeks and was impressed. The Chumash People can't be faulted for wishing things had remained more or less the same before his arrival.

Spanish occupation of the region officially began in 1769. The Presidio was established in 1782 while the American Revolution was raging, Mission San Buenaventura was established in the same year, and the first Santa Barbara Mission in 1786. In 1775, the Spanish had begun making concessions by granting land to retired soldiers. Later, Mexico's successful revolt from Spain in 1821 made Alta California Mexican territory and the new government established an accelerated land grant program for both native-born and naturalized Mexican citizens. The original ranchos were established, and the natives became landless and veritable slaves to the ranchos.

In 1846 the United States invaded Mexico to take Texas, which had far-reaching implications for California as well. Mexico sent Miguel Micheltorena, with a band of questionable soldiers released from jail, to fight to replace Governor Juan Bautista Alvarado and reassert control of the region. Alvarado and his Californio supporters fought off and defeated Micheltorena's forces in Los Angeles in the Battle of Providencia, and California became a state in 1850. This all could have ended very differently; the English and the French had both been eyeing the region as well but seemed to realize that trying to seize control would have been an expensive and difficult endeavor.

The mid-1800s brought gold rush wealth and, with it, a penchant for Victorian architecture. The fashion of this style in all its iterations defined the look of this era. By the 1890s San Francisco builder turned Santa Barbara mayor and city architect Peter J. Barber built the first grand hotel, the Arlington, to welcome wealthy Easterners looking to escape winter back home. Word spread of a pocket of paradise on the California coast tucked between the imposing Santa Ynez mountains and the shimmering Pacific Ocean, where the weather was agreeable year-round. Some of those Easterners built homes here. In 1901, train service became available to and from Los Angeles, connecting the area to the rest of the Southern California region.

Previous Page: The Chapel at El Presidio, 1782, downtown Santa Barbara.

Left and Above: A good example of the work of Alex D'Alfonso, whose modern Mediterranean houses dot the Riviera.

Following Pages: The Gaspar Oreña/Masini adobe. A very early example of the Monterey Colonial style in Southern California.

From the turn of the last century through to the 1940s many of the pedigreed architects of the golden age of American architecture realized exceptional homes and estates in the region. Standouts include Bertram Goodhue, Reginald Johnson, George Washington Smith, Francis Underhill, and Carleton Monroe Winslow. There were others whose accomplishments are not as well-known, however, including the aforementioned Gilded Age architect Peter Barber, G. W. Smith disciple Floyd Brewster, W. Maybury Somervell, Santa Barbara Courthouse architect William Mooser, Joseph Plunkett, Winsor Soule, and others.

There were also builders who were not architects but who had a keen sense of design and an intuitive sense of place who also left an indelible mark on the city. Notably, the Italian American master builder and developer Alessandro (Alex) D'Alfonso, who designed and constructed an impressive collection of buildings and houses, many visible from the street, throughout Santa Barbara that are still standing today. His most quintessential works were the houses he designed for the Diana Lane development, named after his daughter, and a few more special houses just up the hill on the de la Guerra streets, from the 1940s. His particularly inventive amalgam of Mediterranean and modern styes that he referred to as "California Cottages" blend well with the area's signature Spanish Colonial heritage and share a natural flowing floor plan sited to collect great light. Beginning as a cabinetmaker and miniature set designer for Flying A Studios, the Santa Barbara–based silent film studio, he later formed a practice that boasted "every trade under one roof." From 1920 through the 1970s, D'Alfonso designed hotels, restaurants, a chapel at the old mission, and a collection of sought-after homes. Impressively, all of the houses he built prior to 1925 survived the massive earthquake of that year. He designed the streamline moderne Live Oak Dairy building in 1939, with its signature "Old Bossie" cow made by artist Alfred Kuhn perched on its rooftop; he also developed forty acres of Northern Montecito into the coveted development it remains today.

A SANTA BARBARA STYLE

The disaster that was the 1925 earthquake left many of the unreinforced nineteenth-century buildings in ruins. It was also a catalyst for the creation of a unified architectural style that would come to define the city's downtown. For years prior to the quake, civic leaders Bernard and Irene Hoffman along with Pearl Chase and her Plans and Planting Committee of the Community Arts Association had been advocating for the city to officially adopt the Spanish style. The rebuilding effort that followed the earthquake saw city leaders embrace Spanish Revival architecture and, to some degree, Spanish and Italian city planning principles. An architectural board of review was also established in 1925 to oversee uniformity in the redevelopment of the downtown and a first-of-its-kind ordinance was established to back it up. In the 1940s, Carey McWilliams, the eminent journalist and lawyer, in observing this trend toward romanticizing old Spain, coined the phrase "Spanish Fantasy Heritage." That term didn't join the vernacular but remains a good mirror to hold up in judging "authenticity." The Pueblo Viejo Landmark District was established in 1960 to further retain its unique early California Spanish character through careful city planning. While the Spanish style is an idealized reflection of Santa Barbara's past, it nonetheless resulted in an indelible architectural outcome that is now inseparable from the city.

Precedents dating from José de la Guerra's 1849 adobe and later Gaspar Oreña's 1850s addition of a one-and-a-half story house (restored by James Osborne Craig and Mary McLaughlin Craig) still stand in what is now known as the Paseo across the street from City Hall. They are a physical reminder of the area's rich history as well as the core tenets of this architecture: adobe plastered in white, red clay roof tiles accented by decorative wrought iron, and painted decorative tile—all key ingredients that define Spanish Revival style. Casa de la Guerra also demonstrated the ability of its low-slung, thick-walled adobe construction to withstand the effects of the powerful earthquake of 1925.

Inspired by these and other adobes of the region as well as designs introduced by the Moors to Granada and Seville in the thirteenth century, the pioneering architect George Washington Smith was a major influence on perpetuating the Spanish style here. His first house, El Hogar, was built in 1917. Modeled after Andalusian farmhouses he had seen in Spain, the house was already well-known by 1925. Later called the father of the Spanish Colonial Revival, Smith completed over eighty houses in the region as well as the landmark Meridian Studios and the Lobero Theatre with protégé Lutah Maria Riggs.

Along with the Spanish influence on the region, it must be noted that there is a wide and diverse variety of house styles to be found here. There are traditional American farmhouses, turn-of-the-last century Mission Revival and Craftsman, and a number of surviving Queen Anne and Victorian homes around town. Almost anything grows in the fertile soil of these hills, and the architectural climate has always been a productive one as well. Many marvelous examples built over the last century or more survive thanks to the loving care and attention of their owners who take seriously the stewardship of these works of art.

Above: A rare large Claycraft tile frieze depicting the Santa Barbara Mission.

Opposite: A part of El Paseo, a development from the 1920s connecting downtown with El Presidio in the Spanish style. Many notable architects, including James Osborne Craig, Carleton Monroe Winslow, and Lutah Maria Riggs, contributed to the project.

The Early Days

RANCHO SANTA CLARA DEL NORTE
Saticoy, 1837–Today

In the colonial period of California, it was common practice for the Governors of Alta California to grant large tracts of land to loyal citizens, both men and women. These grants encouraged permanent settlement and the ranchos built were sources of agricultural production, providing such staples as beef, beans, and tallow for the towns surrounding the state's missions and presidios. Few of these ranchos survive today, and the land has been subdivided. Historic main posts have been neglected, dismantled, or concretized as museums. In contrast, stewardship and consistent prosperity have enabled Rancho Santa Clara del Norte to evolve and to thrive for nearly two hundred years.

Rancho Santa Clara del Norte has been in the Lloyd-Butler family and their ancestors for over 160 years. In 1862 a small consortium, including Leopoldo Schiappa-Pietra, acquired the drought-stricken 13,988 acres from the original grantee, Juan María Sánchez. Forty years later, and after an extensive probate, Ida Ross, the adopted daughter (and maternal niece) of Leopoldo and his wife, was awarded the 3,000-acre home ranch in 1908, and rights to surface water from the adjacent Santa Clara River. The home ranch remains its prime parcel, strategically located along the southern banks of the river and sheltered from wind by the tip of South Mountain. Ida's grandson, Thomas Lloyd-Butler, his two nephews, and two sons continue to manage and operate the ranch's orchards, pastures, croplands, and its historic main post to this day.

Just as the ranch has evolved through six generations, its farming operations have supported its owners and staff with more consistent and higher value livestock and crops, ranging from grazing animals to lima beans, walnuts, and eventually today's avocados, citrus, and berries. Equally crucial to the ranch's early and consistent success are its fine soil and its unique access to surface water from the Santa Clara River. Early on, surface water drawn from the adjacent river enabled production of higher-value irrigated crops such as sugar beets and lima beans. Further, as early as 1860, the ranch began to sell excess surface water from its lands in the Santa Clara River to farmers on the dry the Oxnard Plain, a substantial and consistent source of income—the Californian equivalent of oil in Texas.

The Schiappa-Pietra, and later the Lloyd-Butler families, have husbanded this bounty with wisdom and creativity. In difficult years, consistent income from water sales maintained financial solvency. In good times, investments were made in new orchards and the rebuilding of the ranch's main post in an elegant way, recalling the grand estates of Schiappa-Pietra's homeland in Italy, which they visited often. By 1900, the humble six-room Sánchez adobe had been tripled in size, including a colonnaded portico and an imposing bifurcated stair capped with a Palladian window. The neatly swept yard was replaced with an Italianate garden with traditional water features and specimen trees, arranged on a central axis. Today, members of the family gather every weekend to work in the office or in the orchards and gardens. Their work and vision enable the ranch to continue to evolve. Collections of objects and curiosities from the natural world have added new layers to the interiors. The gardens now consist of an extensive collection of over 7,000 trees and plants representing 1,200 taxa while unusual new gardens, like the Stumpery, a shade garden set among over 196 logs and tree stumps, add surprise and whimsy. Finally, new orchards, nestled between rows of cover crops and pollinator hedges are laying foundations for growing more nutritious fruit through more sustainable regenerative farming.

Previous Pages:
A guest house amongst a native garden at Rancho Santa Clara del Norte.

Right: Looking down the drive toward orchards in front of the main house.

Right: The formal garden with mature palms.

Left and Above: The formal entry into the living room of the main house.

Opposite and Right: Curiosities from the natural world fill every room in the house and guest house. The current owners' penchant for repaired china and pottery is also evident around the property.

Following Pages: A bird's eye view of the ranch. A lovingly repaired jar.

CALKINS COTTAGE
Santa Barbara, 1896

This quintessential turn-of-the-last-century cottage hidden behind a hedge in downtown Santa Barbara is a private treasure chest of historical *objets*. Many of these items have threads that connect to the region's history while others are family heirlooms collected from around the globe. The owners, multi-generational antiquarians, also have deep roots the area. Consummate locals with encyclopedic knowledge of Santa Barbara's colorful past, they continue a tradition of procuring notable artifacts and enriching the area's heritage by finding good homes for these pieces and paintings.

Left: The elegant but unassuming facade of the cottage belies the treasure trove it contains.

Following Pages: A dizzying array of *objets* and paintings fill the house. The clock is an eighteenth-century patinated bronze figure of a Greek woman. The two patinated bronze putti, from France, are from the early nineteenth century.

Right: A collection of antique portraits, Spanish Colonial silver, and a pair antique Italian reliquaries.

40

Opposite: A large articulated Spanish Colonial Madonna with an eighteenth-century rosary and a collection of Spanish Colonial dippers.

Right: An eighteenth-century chalk portrait above a seventeenth-century French clock of Pan, flanked by two Sèvres cobalt urns.

TWIN PEAKS RANCH
Ojai, 1920–Today

Palmer Sabin, original architect

The town of Ojai, nestled in a bucolic valley south of Santa Barbara, has been a beacon of health and spirituality for hundreds of years. Its modern history began in 1880s when Sherman Day Thacher founded the Thacher School with its ethos "to teach a boy to ride, shoot, and tell the truth." The school grew to become one of the nation's top preparatory academies. At the turn of the century the Foothills Hotel was a top resort destination, drawing well-heeled tourists, including Edward and Florence Libby of the Libby Glass Company in Ohio. The Libbys fell in love with the region and decided to stay and develop a proper town. Libby hired San Diego architects Frank Mead and Richard Requa to design the major parts of downtown in the Spanish Colonial style, including the arcade, post office tower, and the Ojai Valley Inn, originally the Ojai Valley Country Club. Today much of their work remains, giving the area its signature character.

Located on over fifty acres neighboring the Thacher School, Twin Peaks Ranch was established in 1920 with a main residence, three guest houses, and two staff houses designed in the Spanish style by Pasadena architect Palmer Sabin. In addition to a sixty-foot pool and a tennis court, the property includes working buildings such as a stone barn, stables, and a blacksmith shop. There are acres of avocado and citrus trees and a unique landscape design of oaks, sycamores, and eucalyptus as well as cactus and a rose garden.

The owners continue to develop and repurpose sections of the property. They are avid conservationists, having founded the Turtle Conservancy, and host an assurance colony for endangered turtles and tortoises on the ranch.

Right: The original house nestled amongst cats, succulents, and trees.

Below, Center, and Opposite:
One of the many outbuildings that dot the property.
Walls and archways also feature impressive stonework.

Following Pages:
Comfortable ranch style interiors offer a nod to nature and the historic West.

Left: A classic California interior scene.

Above: A noble giant tortoise, one of many that reside in this sanctuary.

Left, Center, and Opposite:
Also in abundance around the property are examples of fine wrought ironwork.

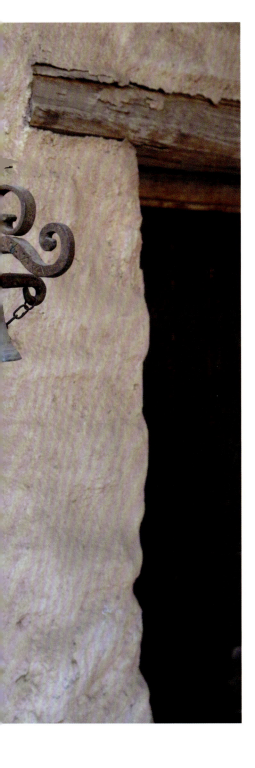

Left: Among the more recent additions to the property is this pool walled in stone.

Spanish Threads

PLAZA RUBIO

Santa Barbara, 1925

Mary McLaughlin Craig, architect

Becker, Henson, Niksto Architects, renovation architects

Kritsada Buajudhavudhivudh, landscape and interior designer

Plaza Rubio, the street named in honor of prominent Franciscan Father José María de Jesús González Rubio, holds a special place in the development of early twentieth-century Santa Barbara. Bordering the southern end of the public lawn and rose garden of the 1812 Santa Barbara Mission lies a gently curved street lined with houses facing the Mission, all with their own personality but sharing a consistent thread of being designed in the complementary Spanish Revival style and adhering to the new city plan for this adopted style. Commissioned by Mrs. J. A. Andrews after the earthquake of 1925, which prompted those in municipal government to legislate reimagining Santa Barbara in the Spanish, these first seven houses became an early small-scale example of American city planning. As noted by architect Stephen Harby, "The houses were sited and massed to create a contextual and complementary setting to the Mission, creating varied massing and roof lines, unified by an alignment of the building line, and minimal interruptions through the use of shared driveways and garages. The street is given a light curve to further inflect towards the Mission."

They were designed by architect Mary McLaughlin Craig, who, along with her architect husband James Osborne Craig, designed many civic and residential buildings that are now familiar and serve as quintessential examples of what many see as the Santa Barbara style.

This house, nearly on axis with the Mission facing north, has a special place in the plan. The arrangement of the rooms in the relatively compact two-thousand-square-foot home provides each with multiple exposures, and the living room has either a window or French doors to the exterior on each of the four walls, achieved through the use of a "U" plan. The extensive renovation, done with the help of architects Peter Becker and Jacob Niksto of Becker, Henson, Niksto Architects (who restored and occupy the last remains of the silent-film-era Flying A Studios), dates from 2015, and its scope was to update building systems and reverse a number of changes made since the original construction. The interior is filled with original art ranging from family portraits of many generations to contemporary watercolors both by the owners and their friends, including Wendy Artin and Alexander Purves. Furnishings range from early American family pieces to English furniture from the sixteenth through the nineteenth century, mostly from the Georgian period.

Previous Pages: Plaza Rubio viewed from the Mission's A.C. Postel Memorial Rose Garden. The yellow roses are named for chef and author Julia Child, a longtime resident.

Left: Though the house is certainly Spanish in style, the furnishings range from early American to English furniture from the sixteenth through the nineteenth centuries.

Following Pages: The breakfast nook.

Previous Pages, Left: Seen on the left, a partial view of a watercolor by Wendy Artin of the Parthenon's frieze, and a watercolor by Alexander Purves on the right.

Previous Pages, Right: Of all the houses on Plaza Rubio, this is the only one that sits directly on axis with the Mission.

Opposite: The dining room.

Right: Peaking through to a guest room.

Left: The cactus garden was designed by Kritsada Buajudhavudhivudh and installed by Brett Faucheaux.

Monterey Colonial

LAS JACARANDAS, RILEY HOUSE

Montecito, 1928

Reginald Johnson, architect

The great early twentieth-century architect Reginald Davis Johnson left a significant body of work in the Santa Barbara region. Not long after his career began in 1911, with a house in Pasadena, he received his first commission in the Santa Barbara area, the 1915 J. Percival Jefferson house, "Miraflores," now well-known as home to the Music Academy of the West. Johnson won many other significant local commissions, from the Clark Estate (Bellosguardo), to the beloved Biltmore Hotel, for which he received the gold medal from the New York Architectural League in 1926. He partnered with two other luminaries in the field Gordon Kaufmann and Roland Coate, early on, and, after the partnership was dissolved, each amicably took individual credit for various projects. Johnson was adept at working in various idioms, designing both grand estates and lasting public work, notably the Santa Barbara Post Office in 1937, an excellent example of the Federal style with elements of both classical and art deco details. The firm collectively is remembered not just for their large-scale work (Kaufmann worked on the Pentagon and on the Hoover Dam), but for human-scale California houses. Johnson's Monterey Colonial homes are noteworthy for their authentic historic facades and elegant Yankee interiors. He was possibly inspired by the still-standing Monterey-style house nearby, located at the edge of Montecito at the base of Ortega Hill, known as the Masini adobe. Rexford Newcomb identifies it in his 1925 book, *The Old Mission Churches and Historic Houses of California*, as the Gaspar Oreña house, linking it to one of the founding fathers of the region.

The architectural historian David Gebhard, interviewed in the *Santa Barbara News Press* in 1987, said, "We don't know when it was built; maybe as early as 1825. It was there by the end of the 1840s." He believed the Monterey style "actually represents a commingling of Hispanic and Anglo architectural traditions influenced by English, French, Spanish and American dwellings in the Caribbean, the American Southeast, the lower Mississippi Delta and the American Southwest. The sources of the Monterey tradition are much more complex than had been realized." The two-story adobe, with overhanging balconies in front and back, is possibly the first of its kind in Southern California.

The Riley House, which Johnson completed in 1928, two years after the Biltmore Hotel, has the qualities one would look for in a Monterey Colonial, including a second-story covered balcony which, like some grander examples, doesn't wrap all the way around the second floor and may be the Caribbean influence Gebhard was referring to, and has no supporting columns and a very clean finish. The smooth stucco walls, combined with little detail around the windows and entry, offer a good balance between the Spanish style and a traditional American house, with the divided pane windows and gracious colonial entry.

Previous Pages: The Riley House with the dramatic backdrop of the Santa Ynez Mountains.

Following Pages: The living room opens directly up to the gracious patio and garden.

Right: A view from the balcony, a standard feature of the Monterey Colonial Style.

Opposite: The house is appointed with traditional American and English furnishings and accented with *objets* and art from Asia.

Right: The fireplace in the den has a fine back-lit Tiffany stained glass wall panel over the mantle.

Left and Above: A lush semitropical garden balanced with pathways and waterways.

MCKEE HOUSE

Montecito, 1926–Today

McNeal Swasey, original architect

Appleton & Associates, restoration/renovation architects

Built on possibly the most iconic beachfront point in the region, this inverted Monterey style courtyard house has enjoyed both the love and labors of its stewards and the efforts of some very significant architectural and landscape design talents. Little is known about its beginnings, but it is believed to be one of the first two houses built on Fernald Point. The point, named after a Santa Barbara city founder, Judge Charles Fernald, is a majestic south-facing knoll that juts into the Pacific Ocean, and is a stone's throw away from the original Gaspar Oreña house—which is now cut off from the beach by the modern highway, but would have been just a short walk down the hill through the 1920s. There is an underground fresh water source as well, which allows for a guilt-free lawn abutting the sand, which the other original houses on the Point were known for in the early days.

The house was originally designed by architect McNeal Swasey, who had worked for the notable architect Myron Hunt. Architect Lutah Maria Riggs had a hand in an early remodel of the house in the early 1950s, though it is not clear if her work is still extant. Renowned contemporary architect Marc Appleton was first introduced to the property in 1994 but it wasn't until 2008, when the current owners purchased the property, that he was enlisted to undertake both major renovations and minor additions to the entire first and second floors. The interior changes included adding a bar to the library and a new kitchen. Extensive exterior work was done as well, especially on the terraces and throughout the grounds. On the beach side, a spa was added, and the original beach cabana was rehabilitated.

Beloved landscape architect Eric Nagelmann is responsible for the array of palms, including the remarkable Caryota gigas in the courtyard and others around the property. He also designed the serene koi pond and trellised walkway. His gardening talents and contributions to the community as a whole are well-known.

Left and Following Pages:: A bird's eye view from the courtyard to the Pacific. The giant Strelitzia birds-of-paradise were already mature, and inspired Eric Nagelmann to continue with the subtropical style of the landscape design. The Monterey Colonial elements of the house are turned inward toward the courtyard, framing four magnificent Caryota fishtail palms. Aeonium circle the fountain, carved from native sandstone, in the center of the entry courtyard.

Pages 80–81: Glass-paned walls framing the Pacific Ocean.

Opposite, Above, and Right: A view into the living room. To the right, the entry hall, then the dining room with a contemporary painting of Fernald Point.

Following Pages: The amazing trees, including the unique pollarded native sycamores, atop this property are its true landmarks.

Pages 86–87: Howea palms flank the koi pond, connected to a trellised outdoor room resplendent with wisteria.

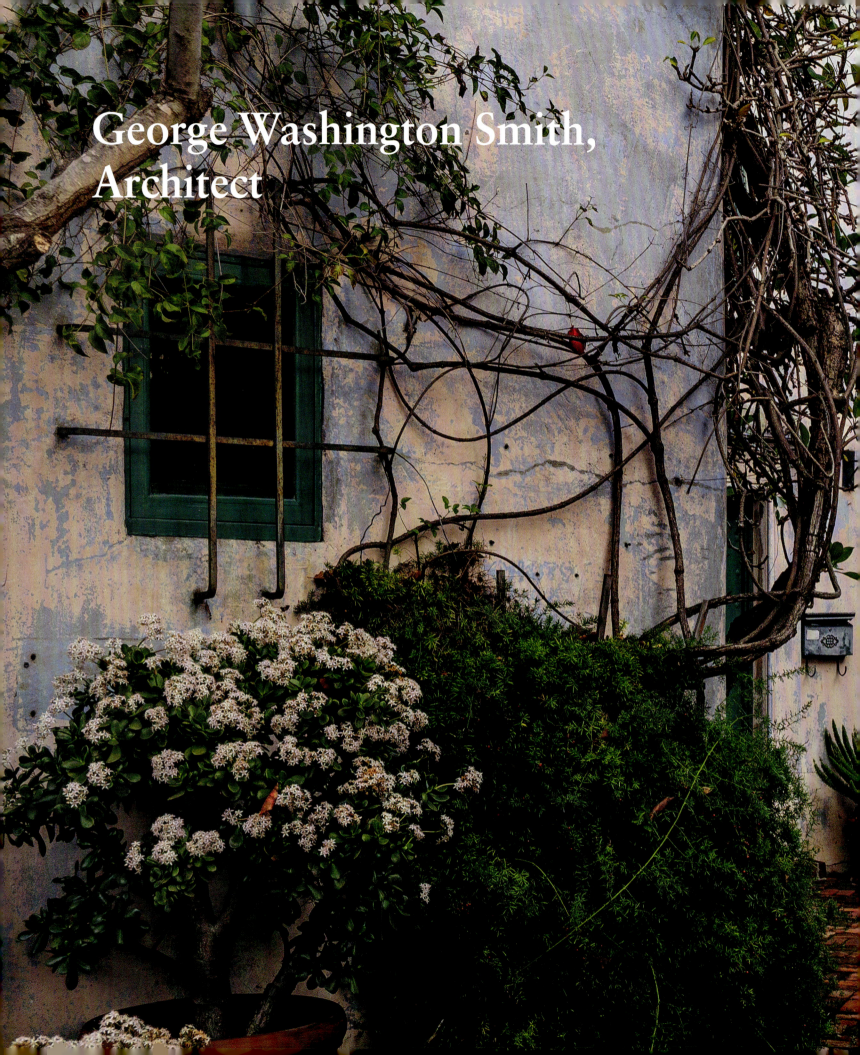

George Washington Smith, Architect

George Washington Smith and His Legacy

by Douglas Woods

No single architect has left a more indelible imprint on the Santa Barbara region than George Washington Smith. A self-made man who studied painting at the Pennsylvania Academy of Fine Arts as well as in Paris and Rome, he had success as a plein air artist, including exhibiting at the Panama-Pacific International Exposition in San Francisco in 1915. After some years spent as a bachelor in Santa Barbara, he married Mary Catherine Greenough, and they purchased their first property in what was then the rural town of Montecito. By the end of 1918, and despite materials shortages due to the Great War, he had completed his first house, a design based on the Andalusian farmhouses he had seen while traveling in Spain. He named it Casa Dracaena, though it became known as El Hogar. With its blend of white stucco walls, and decorative tile and ironwork, El Hogar evoked a romantic, perhaps idealized, era that offered an escape to the old world yet allowed enjoyment of the amenities of modern life in America, an appealing notion for many looking to establish homes in the post–World War I era. The house became a template for many more to come.

His early homes were widely published in architecture journals and used in brochures for building materials, and he became well-known around the country for popularizing the Spanish Colonial Revival style. Many residential commissions followed. Thanks to the varied tastes of his expanding client base, Smith was offered the opportunity to explore other idioms, including Cottage and Tudor, as well as elaborate Moorish-style designs, at which he proved to be adept. His Spanish houses, however, remain his signature. Perhaps the most famous one is Casa del Herrero, or the House of the Blacksmith, built for industrialist George Fox Steedman, and now preserved as a house museum. He was awarded numerous public commissions, and his work is well represented around downtown Santa Barbara. Such buildings as the Santa Barbara News-Press building, Meridian Studios, and the Lobero Theatre, which he designed along with his protégé Lutah Maria Riggs, all stand today and are cited as references against which to judge contemporary building proposals for the downtown area.

Previous Pages: The courtyard of Meridian Studios.

Opposite and Above: The Meridian Studios, designed by George Washington Smith in 1923, were designed and built as artist's studios. Commissioned by modern civic leader Bernard Hoffman, they sit on the northern part of the property behind the 1830 Lugo adobe—one of El Presidio's oldest—which Hoffman acquired and preserved.

Smith died at fifty-four in 1930, ending a short but prolific and highly influential career. His memory lives on in the public sphere in no small part thanks to Dr. David Gebhard of UC Santa Barbara, who was a champion of the architect and his work. In 1964, as director of the University Art Museum, he organized an exhibition, accompanied by a catalogue, devoted to Smith with the assistance of Lutah Maria Riggs. He also initiated the Architectural Drawings Collection at UCSB, where Smith's papers reside along with many others. Dr. Gebhard's wife, Patricia, continued this legacy after his death by writing the major monograph on George Washington Smith in 2005.

Above and Opposite: The Steedman House, better-known as Casa del Herrero, which Smith designed and built between 1922 and 1925, is the most recognizable and referenced landmark in his oeuvre. It stands today as a well-maintained house museum and a definitive example of his Spanish Colonial Revival work.

Following Pages: The living room.

CANBY, CUNNINGHAM HOUSE

Montecito, 1922–1925

George Washington Smith, architect

Stephen Geiszler, restoration/renovation architect

Smith initially designed this house, tucked away on a flat lot in Montecito, for his wife's cousin James Canby in 1922. Canby lived in the house for only three years before he sold it to Edith Cunningham, a widow from Boston. Cunningham had a grander vision for the house and commissioned Smith to return in 1925 do extensive work that included adding a library, a primary suite, and additional maid's rooms, and enlarging the dining room. The house is one of the finest examples of Smith's signature Spanish-style work, with antique and handcrafted tile, carved mahogany doors, and extensive wrought iron fixtures and grilles. Smith angled the Cunningham additions off of the original house in four directions, resulting in an unconventional floor plan in which arched halls lead to the various rooms, each with their own surprising character. The wooden beamed ceilings express a simple geometry that contrast with the more intricate paneling found throughout the house, except in the library, which has a finely detailed hand-carved vaulted ceiling and an impressive iron chandelier. Smith designed the fountain that anchors the far end of the property with an eight-pointed-star pond and Persian tile.

In recent years the house was tastefully updated by architect Steve Geiszler, who undertook a three-year remodel that brought the house up to twenty-first-century standards while faithfully preserving the timeless quality and the soul of George Washington Smith's work.

Right: The inviting approach to the entrance.

Above: The living room.

Right: Deeply carved woodwork punctuates the hallway doors and the shutters of a comfortable window nook seating area.

Opposite and Right: Additional examples of the craftsmanship Smith employed include elaborate woodwork; excellent ironwork, such as in this chandelier; and tile work, seen recessed here.

Following Pages: A delightful garden view from an upper bedroom.

Pages 104–105: One the ground level, the house opens up to the garden on all sides.

ISHAM HONEYMOON COTTAGE AND NATATORIUM

Carpinteria, 1920–1928

Located in the beachside community of Sandyland in Carpinteria, the Isham property demonstrates Smith's deft abilities designing in styles other than the strictly Spanish. Wealthy Chicago businessman Albert K. Isham initially commissioned a beach house in 1920, which Smith designed in a spare French Norman style. By 1927 Isham had purchased an additional two-and-a-half acres with the intention of building a gymnasium and pool house. Isham had travelled to Morocco, where he had become enamored with Moorish architecture and he asked Smith to redesign the entrance and living room of the house in the Moorish style and to design the entire athletic facility in the same style. Smith constructed an elaborate natatorium with a traditional white-walled exterior capped with a ziggurat roofline. Massive wooden doors fill a tiled keyhole arch surround at the entrance, which leads into a dazzling building containing a twenty-by-sixty-foot pool topped with a retractable roof. Though the tile could be mistaken for Tunisian, it is actually American, made by Gladding, McBean. The two impressive tile murals at either end are the work of the Malibu Potteries. Though North African details are found in other Smith homes, this "casbah" is the only example of Smith working purely in the Islamic style.

At some point Smith was commissioned by Isham to build a smaller French Norman cottage that came to be known as the Honeymoon Cottage. He kept this design more traditional inside, employing exquisitely fitted clear fir paneling on the walls and ceiling, where not one nail can be seen.

Isham's parties were legendary; he entertained the Hollywood crowd—who were often on their way to William Randolph Hearst's castle in San Simeon—at the pool house. Isham died in 1931 at the age of thirty-eight, and the property was left derelict for many years. In the 1930s, a violent Pacific storm washed away four of the estate's original seven acres and wrecked the main house. The Honeymoon Cottage and natatorium, however, survived unscathed.

Left: The charming entrance to the Honeymoon Cottage.

Left: Superb craftsmanship exemplified by the handsome geometric pattern of the wood paneling. No nails are visible on the walls or ceiling.

Above: Bowling pins, relics from the old bowling alley, serve as a reminder of recreation of the past.

Opposite: The porch on a peaceful day.

Folllowing Pages: Ocean view from the Honeymoon Cottage.

Right: The entry approach to the natatorium, with a stylized onion-arched entry surrounded by tile, the massing balanced by a dome and tower.

Opposite and Above: The interior is surprisingly elaborate, from the tile and large antique casbah lamps to the repeated loops of the horseshoe arches and the impressive carved vaulted dome circled at the base by widows.

Following Pages: A pair of retractable skylights cover the pool to offer protection from the elements and to provide natural light.

Smith's Continuing Influence

CASA DE LEON
Santa Barbara Riviera, 1964–Today

It seems fitting that this impeccable Andalusian-style hillside house was once the home of David Gebhard's publisher, Gibbs Smith. Though not designed by George Washington Smith, the home is yet another example of the Mediterranean influence that he brought to the region. The multistory structure sits high on a steep hill with sweeping views from the Riviera past downtown Santa Barbara below and past the waterfront to the Channel Islands. Once neglected, it has been meticulously renovated and restored, with its current owners lovingly adding details throughout that Smith surely would have applauded. Built in 1964 by an architect who salvaged bits and parts of old homes from the 1920s and '30s and incorporated them into the design, the house was never fully realized. In 2014 the current owners purchased it from Gibbs Smith and set out on a five-year journey to bring the house to its current glory. They studied the work of George Washington Smith and his protégé, Lutah Maria Riggs, for inspiration. The owners had previous experience in historic restoration but this was the first "re-creation" they had done. The result is a 1964 house brought back to 1929.

Much time was spent finding treasures for the interior as well as specifying fabrics, lighting, and finishes, both inside and out. The house, adorned with custom ironwork and tile, also features the last private residential decorative painting commission by Colette Cosentino.

Previous Pages: A California garden scene.

Right: A dream realized in the hills of the Santa Barbara Riviera.

Following Pages: A wide arch connects a quintessential indoor/outdoor living room to a cozy sunken den.

Opposite: The dining room, with its unadorned groin-vaulted ceiling, allows for the appreciation of pure geometry while the mirrors open up the space and bring the outside in.

Above: A cozy nook in the indoor loggia.

Right: A cutting garden displays excellent stone masonry.

Above and Opposite: The terraced lot allows the guest house to be close to the main house while maintaining privacy for both. Details large and small abound, from the water garden protecting the guest house entry to the decorative arts found throughout.

Following Pages: The back patio offers paths and steps, inviting one to explore the hillside in every direction.

CASA DE SEVILLE

Montecito, 2005

Nils Holroyd Design, architectural design and construction

Designed by Nils Holroyd in 2005 as a nod to the Steedman estate known as Casa del Herrero (House of the Blacksmith), George Washington Smith's best-known work, this home is rooted in timeless historicism. Holroyd, early in his career as an architectural designer in the 1980s, was deemed by David Gebhard as "one to watch." He built this house from the ground up, influenced by Smith, and succeeded in creating and maintaining a level of detail and authenticity not often seen in contemporary attempts at designing a classic Spanish Colonial.

Quietly sited behind thick walls and a large wooden gate that seals the arched entry from the street outside into the motor court, the whitewashed house sits among an oasis of gardens and outdoor dining and entertaining areas. The lucky couple who own the home contributed their own talents to continue the evolution of its design; he has been a passionate gardener from a young age, and she is a talented and highly informed designer. She created a jewel-box interior that is endlessly visually rich yet also comfortable and fun for family—and larger—gatherings. It is evident that their ambitious interior project, which reflects both devotional and regal Spanish elements and includes an ornate office in the Moorish style tucked away at one end of the living area, was a labor of love. The office, referred to as the casbah, was inspired by, among other things, Doris Duke's Shangri La and the work of designer Serdar Gülgün. For the gardens they collaborated with Bay Area designer Davis Dalbok of Living Green Design, adding a palm garden surrounding a seating area replete with commissioned hand-carved Indian marble garden furnishings.

Left: The approach to the classic Spanish Colonial elevation with stone mosaic crosshatching in the motor court.

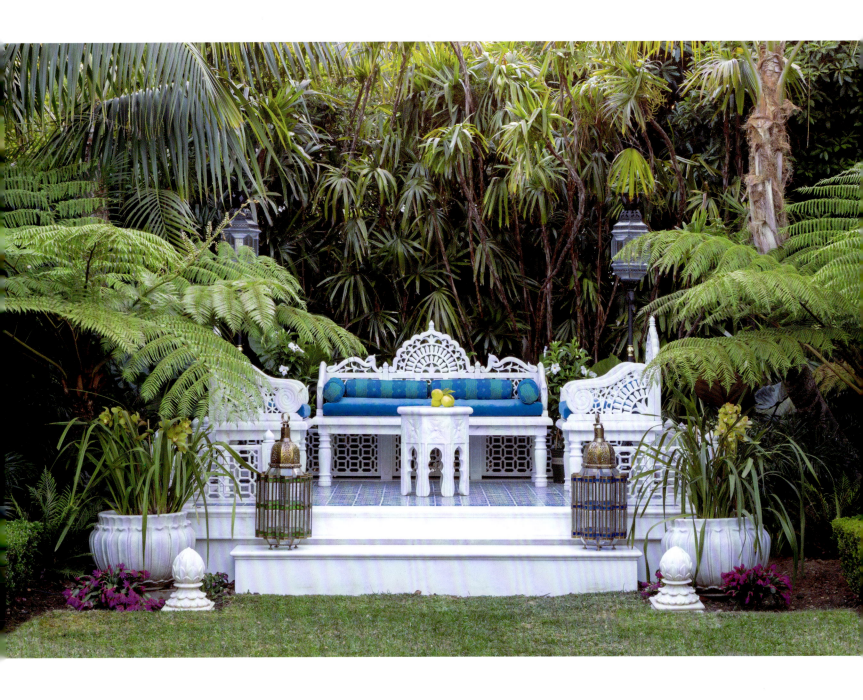

Above: Indian garden furniture, hand-carved in marble, forms the focal point of the tropical garden.

Opposite: The living room, whose Spanish Colonial artifacts and furnishings revolve around Peruvian paintings of the Virgin, is both graceful and contemplative.

Following Pages: Light and breeze merge the interiors with the gardens.

Page 136: The landing with a deeply scalloped window.

Pages 137–138: The dining room, painted in warm tones with a decoratively edged groin vault, opens to the outside. The courtyard garden.

Gardens in Paradise

GARDENS IN PARADISE
by M. Brian Tichenor

In the coastal region we now know as Santa Barbara, the attractions of the landscape span millennia. Linguists believe the Chumash people, who husbanded the land and sea there before European contact, most likely have been in residence for upwards of ten thousand years. The abundance and breadth of available foodstuffs, coupled with a reliably mild climate, made for an astonishingly stable cultural environment. Once they came, they stayed.

Similarly, in the time of the missions, the nearly perfect setting of the nascent town led to it being the most important administrative outpost in the southern section of Alta California, during both the Spanish and Mexican periods. The rapid success of the "mission package" of European plants that accompanied the padres attested to latent possibilities that a bit of irrigation could bring to such a place.

In the later nineteenth century, with Americanization came echoes of the growing national interest in ornamental gardening. Santa Barbara, early on a highly regarded "wintering" destination for wealthy Easterners, attracted and supported some very ambitious nursery establishments, necessary adjuncts to the houses being built for the new influx of California enthusiasts arriving every year. Horticultural sophistication perhaps reached its apex with the work of the erudite and influential Francesco Franceschi. When he first arrived in the small town in 1893, he immediately ascertained its tremendous potential. It was an ideal natural setting, perfect for the scientific plant propagation laboratory he envisioned, thanks to the salubrious Mediterranean climate and its south-facing mountain range fronting the cool Pacific Ocean. No place he had seen in his travels had so evoked his native Italy. Part of what impressed him was the already significant plantings that notable nurserymen such as Joseph Sexton and Kinton Stevens had populated the area with; they had shown that virtually anything, apart from those plants that required a freeze, could grow there. Santa Barbara was, from its very beginnings, a plantsman's paradise and it was to play a prominent role in the propagation of plants for trade around the globe. Franceschi, in his twenty years in Santa Barbara, was at the center of the worldwide acclimatization movement. His deeply researched catalogues of successful Santa Barbara plantings and exhaustively detailed accounts of the suitability of imported perennials from around the world paved the way for a growing community that would increasingly reflect this highly cosmopolitan planting palette. So much of the early garden tradition of the region reflects this transformational recognition of the possibilities of the luxuriant, exotic garden that was possible to achieve in this, the only climate of its kind in the United States. We see echoes of this enthusiasm in the 140-year-old remnants of the Kinton Stevens Tanglewood nursery, which underlay the extraordinary grounds of Lotusland, in the exuberant celebration of form at Aloes in Wonderland.

Significantly, the maturation of this horticultural bonanza yielded a period of garden-making that defined the traditions we see in this book. Winifred Starr Dobyns, the noted American suffragist, landscape designer, and author of *California Gardens* (1931), describing the 1920s, wrote: "Overnight, palaces and villas seem to spring into being on barren hills and in wooded canyons. Within a short year, a garden will blossom where yesterday only greasewood and scrub oak clothed the ground. Wealth and art together have been employed to lay out many of California's gardens." Given its unique setting and a cultural milieu that had drawn a particularly well-educated and well-traveled population to this "American Riviera," Santa Barbara and its environs were the stage for the emergence of a remarkable Californian vision of the Mediterranean garden that would reach its apex in the 1920s. This seminal and highly adaptable aesthetic, so well suited to both the climate and mythology of the place, flourishes to this day.

The beauty of this coast has attracted generations of artists, and in the early twenties, concurrent with the first great expression of this garden movement, a serendipitous coalition of like-minded residents formed, with a grant from the Carnegie Institute and a mandate to explore four branches of cultural pursuits, the Santa Barbara Community Arts Association. Happily, one branch was Plans and Plantings, whose stated goal was to provide guidance for the beautification of the city

Previous Pages: The gardens of Las Jacarandas.

Above: The entrance to the stumpary at Rancho Santa Clara del Norte.

Right: The gardens of Aloes in Wonderland, where one will find hundreds of aloes, agave, cactus, and succulents as well as the largest known private garden of cycads, seen here being propagated.

Left: The Aloes in Wonderland overlooking Summerland.

Following Pages: The original Olive Allée dating to the original Peter Reidel plantings with a lane introduced by Eric Nagelmann.

by developing proposals for ideal projects—city street studies, harbor developments, small cottages, parks and treescapes. Their workshops yielded a remarkable vision for the growing city, backed up by serious, detailed plans and evocative renderings. In this moment, after the success of Bertram Goodhue's greatly admired California-Panama exhibition in San Diego, there was an aspiration to create an appropriate "Southern California Style." Much was written, and proposals were being made throughout the region, but what cemented the success of Santa Barbara's efforts in this regard was the dramatic and disastrous earthquake of 1925. It leveled the city, and in its place, this carefully considered vision of a Spanish-inflected town-in-a-garden was built.

There is one figure who plays an outsized role in this formative decade. As historian David Gebhard noted: "George Washington Smith was one of the first of the major California architects to conceive of the close relationship between the building itself and the gardens, drive, and open spaces around it." His houses and gardens, almost from the moment they were built, struck a chord with a population seeking an authentic expression of place. His careful painter's eye, trained in the current trends of Paris and New York, took the Andalusian house and garden and imbued it with a modern sense of clarity and syncopation. His gardens were inextricable parts of his compositions. In his own words: "In the Spanish Garden, the long open vista of the Italian Garden is transformed into a vista through many gateways so that the feeling of intimacy and mystery is achieved, rather than an effect of formality and grandeur. One is never overcome by seeing it all at once, but one has new surprises as he progresses through the garden." This sense of mystery, crossed with the more modest scale of the grounds of even grand twentieth-century homes, was recognized as a brilliant method for enhancing the extraordinary natural settings into which these gardens were built.

George Washington Smith was responsible for several of the projects in this book, but more broadly, the house-and-garden strategies he pioneered inform many of the gardens we see here. Smith considered the garden as an integral part of the architectural plan, and as such, its hardscape serves as a literal extension of the house, a strategy that would come to characterize the period and style. Regarding the architect's own house, Elizabeth de Forest recalled: "It was an inspiration for scores of other Santa Barbara gardens made in the Spanish style, with its tall trees, the paths and beds laid out symmetrically, all in straight lines, emphasized by edgings of dwarf box, sunlight and shadow playing over an oblong sunken pool on the terrace."

Many of the finest Santa Barbara gardens of the early twentieth century share this close affiliation between house plan and garden plan: at Casa Bienvenida by Addison Mizner or Carleton Winslow's Billings Estate, we see the dynamics and strength of the architect's syntax for the house projected into the garden: the full realization of the work of art would arguably be lost in the absence of the garden architecture. In others, such as Francis Underhill's remarkable Arcady, the architectonic garden language, refined and abstract, is of greater importance, in its original form, than the buildings. Similar strong axial interventions organize the plan of what is now Lotusland; these elements were designed and executed in the twenties, in its middle iteration, when the garden was known as Cuesta Linda. In a sense, it is these formal armatures that provide the structure into which the exuberance of Ganna Walska's eccentric gardens are set, leading to a very compelling dialogue.

The long history of gardens in this region is characterized by a deep connection to the natural beauties of the place, and to the nearly limitless breadth of plants that thrive in its coastal plain and hillsides; this yields what we see in these pages—a heritage of devoted garden-making, inflected with curiosity and refinement—an American Riviera indeed.

LOTUSLAND

Montecito, 1882–1920

Reginald Johnson, George Washington Smith, architects

Peter Riedel, Ralph Kinton Stevens, Lockwood de Forest Jr.
Joseph Knowles, Eric Nagelmann, and others

In 1882, pioneering nurseryman and palm enthusiast Ralph Kinton Stevens began assembling a huge collection of trees on this thirty-seven-acre property, which served as his home as well as his commercial nursery, known as Tanglewood. Stevens planted many significant trees that now dominate the landscape and form the bones of what would evolve into the eclectic landmark garden that it is today. Upon his passing, his widow maintained the property, eventually selling it to Erastus Palmer Gavit and his wife, Marie. The Gavits formalized the estate, commissioning architect Reginald Johnson to build a new main house in the Spanish Colonial Revival style, and added subsequent buildings and add-ons by architect George Washington Smith. Working with garden designer Peter Riedel, Gavit continued the tradition of garden development at the estate, renamed Cuesta Linda, adding a swimming pool on axis with a grand cypress allée, among other features.

Thanks to the efforts of several subsequent landscape visionaries, and most notably, Lotusland's patron saint, Madame Ganna Walska, who purchased the estate in 1941, the garden has grown beyond its foundational origins and has evolved into an eclectic and wondrous botanical garden recognized as one of the top ten gardens in the world.

Right: The pool house by George Washington Smith now guards the lotus pond.

Following Pages: The approach with the now-mature cactus gardens.

Left: Original opposing tiled benches face each other on axis past the lotus pond through to the Cypress Allée, punctuated at the end by a wishing well.

Following Pages: Under an old oak and past another part of the cactus grove, the eye gets lost in the lush wonders beyond.

Other Idioms

PARAÍSO IMAGINADO

Santa Barbara, 1995

Bobby Webb and Joey Webb, architecture and landscape design

It took tenacity and vision to bring this wondrous tropical paradise to reality. After driving many miles for many years around the area in the 1990s in search of a perfect property to build a retreat, Eden was finally found buried deep in a canyon in Santa Barbara. Thankfully, the owner, a well-known designer of luxury estates in the Santa Barbara area, was able to see past the challenges before him. The property was an abandoned horse ranch left derelict, with neglected structures amongst old power lines and vehicles on blocks littering the property. Undaunted, he took on the task of removing all the debris, restoring the creek, and laying out a magical collection of gardens that include a waterfall and lake set among a collection of palms, gingers, and a variety of subtropical plants as well as a formal rose garden with arbors modeled after the famous Phipps Estate and Old Westbury Gardens on Long Island, New York. The owner, a passionate supporter of birds, devoted sizable portions of the sprawling sixty-acre property to forty enclosures housing his collection of endangered birds that he nurtures and breeds in order to reduce the need for collectors to seek them from the wild.

A wooden bridge leads over one of three ponds set among pampas grass and papyrus to the house, which was designed to be open to nature in all directions and is inspired by a movie set of an imagined *plantación* in Cuba. The red-tin-roofed Caribbean-style plantation house has an inviting wraparound veranda, shuttered windows, and ornate wood detailing. Inside, delicate Victorian fretwork accents the doorways and Indian architectural wood fragments are especially dramatic against perfect sage green walls. The primary suite opens up to its private koi pond with waterfalls actually bringing the natural world into the house. Immersed in this oasis, with the caws of exotic birds in the distance and a seemingly endless backdrop of swaying palms and old oaks, one quickly forgets that one is just a few miles from downtown Santa Barbara and the rest of civilization.

Previous Pages: A bridge to paradise.

Right: Paradise reflected in a pond; the imagined Caribbean comes to life.

Following Pages: The elegant living room.

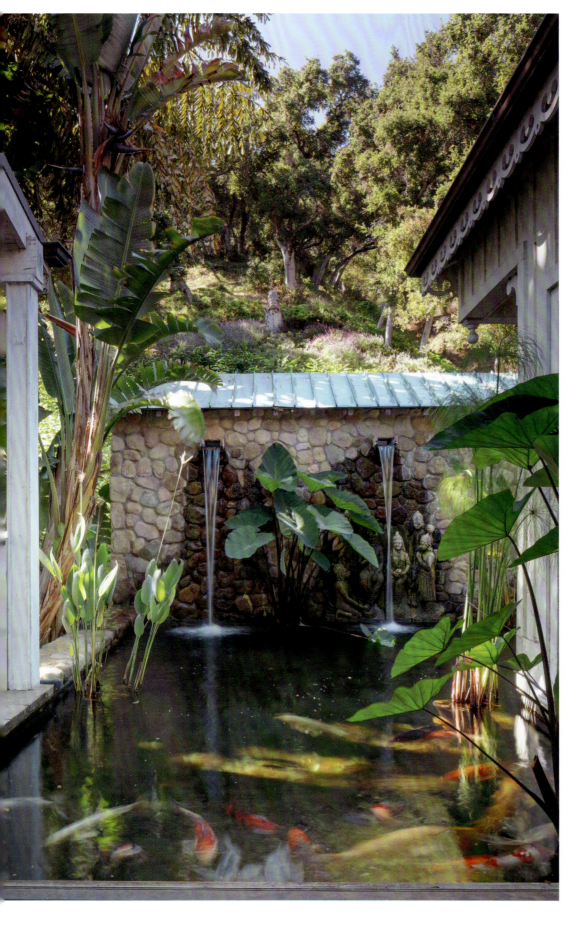

Previous Pages: The outdoors literally meets the indoors where the serene koi pond and primary suite join.

Left: The rose garden.

Following Pages: A waterfall oasis. Flamingos roam the wondrous property.

Pages 168–169: May all beings everywhere be happy and free.

MONTECITO CREOLE

Montecito, 1971

A. Hays Town, architect

Architect A. Hays Town is not a household name in Southern California, let alone the American West. In the American South, however, he is well-known as a quintessential regionalist whose authentic Creole houses are beloved. Early in his career he worked in various historic idioms, from the Federal style to modernism, but eventually his sole focus became designing gracious French American houses that refined the definition of a great Louisiana house. Honoring the Creole tradition, a vernacular that grew out of old New Orleans, Town's deep knowledge and understanding of the region's architectural roots, cultivated over many decades, is evident in his work. Inspired by the best plans of the French Quarter and the great houses of Baton Rouge, his homes are functional, and they weather well. His integration of house and garden, utilizing forecourts and courtyards to access to the outdoors wherever possible, sets the stage for an enviable and gracious indoor/outdoor lifestyle so well suited to Southern California.

This is Town's only California house, on an idyllic hillside in Montecito. The topography was different than the typical flat lots he was used to designing on so it's a unique example of his work. The two-and-a-half-story home has a traditional walled forecourt at the entrance where one is greeted by a fountain, and a classic wide facade with tall, shuttered windows on either side of the centered front door, but he deviates from the traditional floor plan as the house is staggered on the slope. The motor court is approached from the side and leads to the garages at the bottom of the house, situated where one might imagine the basement. Shaded walkways reminiscent of alleys in the French Quarter lead around the house past antique French Biot olive oil jars, lanterns, and the house's louvered shutters. A requisite *pigeonaire* is tucked away in the lush garden, which was designed by Louisiana landscape architect Michael Hopping, who worked with Town on the plans. The entire property exudes an authentic sense of historicism and charm.

Left: A splendid Creole house enveloped by its garden.

Right: The living room with a traditional brick fireplace painted white, and French doors opening to the porch and gardens beyond.

Following Pages: The dining room. The foyer with a special second-story opening as a nod to the French Quarter of New Orleans.

Left: A different view of the entryway.

Above: The courtyard entrance column capital, a nod to a Charleston heritage next to bougainvillea.

Right: On the patio, orchids and a collection of antique architectural panels featuring flowers and birds from Thailand.

Following Pages: The lush, sloped garden.

MONTALBA
Summerland, 1995

A house that was built in 1995 that could be carbon-dated as centuries old is a special thing. What has been built here represents an accumulation of the great eras of architectural history, from ancient Rome to the Spanish Colonial era. It is not done in a "style." It is a celebration of Classicism, and, its various iterations' abilities to combine these ages in unity. Its erudite owners are a Classical and Medieval scholar and a renowned photographer. After spending much time strolling their empty land considering siting and how to lay out the house and gardens, they arrived at want they wanted—a new house that looks old, as if it had been here for several hundred years. Their idea was to create accurate classical detail using rustic materials instead of marble. They employed striped masonry, a take on *opus vittatum* (banded work), a technique popular in ancient Rome. To that end, they incorporated old materials and antique architectural elements such as seventeenth-century limestone fireplaces found in France and eighteenth-century Spanish doors procured from various auctions and dealers. The oldest elements are two thirteenth-century marble portals from Portugal that a friend alerted them to that were being offered for sale by a collector who had purchased them forty years prior from the William Randolph Hearst warehouses. They also created outdoor rooms among the gardens and between structures, connecting the plan for people to enjoy in such a way so that they don't feel swallowed by the enormous expanse before them. They enlisted architect Don Nulty, who graciously acquiesced to their exacting plans and helped realize their dream. This included incorporating materials from the centuries to house art and allow the house to meet today's building codes.

    The overall result of their now-realized vision is a transportive home imbued with soul. It is easy to say that when there, the outside world drifts away. This is true, but more to the point, when there, time drifts away. Being surrounded by both the calm and consequence of history embodied in art and architecture, one is reminded of the gravity of these things. Everything about this home is a reminder that our built environment is a reflection of who we are, and who we were.

Right: The bell tower of Sunrise Mountain with an old wellhead in the courtyard.

Right: The living room with its combination of seventeenth- and eighteenth-century appointments at home with the owners' contemporary art.

Following Pages: An impressive massing of art and decorative arts from throughout the ages.

Left: The dining room features a collection of seventeenth-century Madonnas from Peru.

Above: A cooks' kitchen from centuries past, completely functional today.

Opposite: A dignified friend, Onesto, in his quality stable. The Doric columns in this stable are modeled after those from an old estancia in Colombia. The Spanish eighteenth-century doors at the end lead to an artist's studio.

Followiing Pages: An outdoor room amidst citrus.

Page 190: A thirteenth-century door surround frames a seventeenth-century Madonna.

Page 191: An apse on the west side of the house is a great contemporary example of ancient Roman bandwork, or *opus vittatum*.

Left: The pool and guest house with the Santa Barbara Waterfront in the distance.

Following Pages: Olive trees frame the view toward the paddocks and the ocean beyond.

Pages 196–197: A view from the teahouse toward Casa Bienvenida.

Great Estates

BILLINGS ESTATE

Eucalyptus Hill, 1926, 1996 (restoration and renovation), 2019 (landscape redesign)

Carleton Monroe Winslow, architect

Michael DeRose, restoration and renovation architect

P. Nicolas Raubertas, landscape redesign and additional interior architecture

Another of many a phoenix to rise in Santa Barbara after the 1925 earthquake, what was once a 1919 Francis T. Underhill villa then lost, was replaced by a splendid Spanish Colonial Revival home designed by Carleton Monroe Winslow in 1929. Winslow was a master of the style and already had a prolific career. He was instrumental in designing the influential 1915 Panama-California Exposition in San Diego, along with Bertram Goodhue (who designed El Fureidis—the first of the great estates of the early twentieth century in the area), which ushered in the national romance with the Spanish Revival fantasy.

The client was a master in his own right—a master of industry. Cornelius Kingsley Garrison Billings was a co-founder of what became Union Carbide. He, along with co-founder George Owen Knapp, developed two of the other great estates in the area. An influential donor to various important local artistic and civic institutions, including the region's hospital system, Billings was an avid yachtsman, horseman, and horse breeder. He hosted a famous 1903 dinner party attended by thirty-six guests on horseback in New York City, and in 1909 he and his exceptional horse Lou Dillon were given a Fabergé kovsh, or loving cup, by Tsar Nicholas in recognition of their record-breaking victory in a Moscow harness race. A street just off the greens of the Montecito Country Club named after Lou Dillon still runs down the hill from where her stable once stood on the 180-acre estate. (Among other significant architectural and engineering achievements Billings commissioned is an impressive arcade, featuring Guastavino arches, now at Fort Tryon Park in New York City.)

The Billings Estate, perched at the top of Eucalyptus Hill overlooking the Pacific and the Channel Islands beyond, was headed toward ruin when it was saved by its current stewards in 1992. They lovingly restored the estate and gardens with the help of respected local architectural designer Michael DeRose, who tracked down the original plans at UC Santa Barbara and enhanced the deign with his vision and attention to detail. Later, designer P. Nicolas Raubertas was enlisted to redesign the gardens that had suffered from years of drought. He also designed the formal Moorish-inspired approach, featuring roses and a Moroccan-style tiled fountain. The current owners, like Billings, are philanthropists who support the arts and various local causes. Today the estate retains the noble presence, and Winslow would certainly approve.

Left: The entry from the motor court with the new rose gardens.

Following Pages: The back entry to the garden.

Left: The dining room.

Above: The stairwell shares the same level of elaborately carved woodwork as the dining room and the mantle in the living room.

Right: Note the stenciled ceiling.

Opposite: The courtyard on the west, shown in the beautiful afternoon light.

Above: The incredible view of Bellosguardo and beyond from the promontory.

Following Pages: The rose garden framed by the colonnade and bougainvillea.

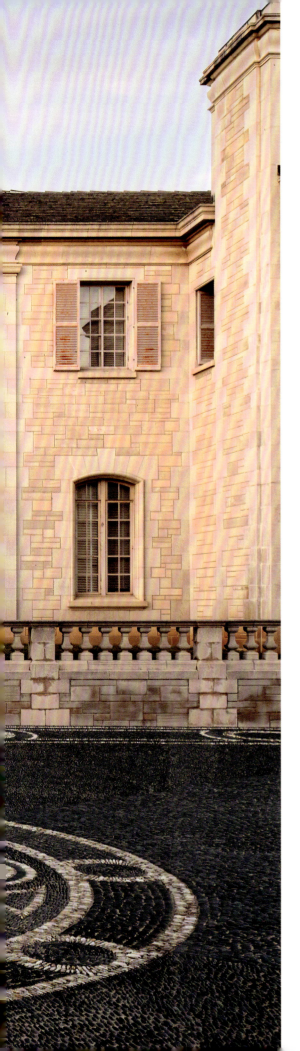

BELLOSGUARDO, CLARK ESTATE
Santa Barbara, 1936
Reginald Johnson, architect

Yet another of Santa Barbara's great homes that owes its existence in no small part to the watershed event that was the earthquake of 1925, Bellosguardo enjoys a rich and mysterious history. Meaning "beautiful lookout" and with its one-thousand feet of beach frontage, the estate was named by the property's original owners in 1902, who lived there in an ornate Italianate villa for two decades. They ultimately sold the property to self-made copper baron William Clark. Clark, in addition to being a senator, was a charitable patron of the arts who, among other things, founded the Los Angeles Philharmonic orchestra, was a well-known collector of rare books, and whose art bequest is core to the collection in the National Gallery. He and his wife Anna had two daughters, Andrée, who died young, and Huguette.

Clark died in his lavish gilded age Fifth Avenue mansion in New York City in 1925, three months before the earthquake that changed the face of Santa Barbara, never able to enjoy Bellosguardo. With the original house damaged, Anna hired architect Reginald Johnson to build a new home that reflected her more restrained taste. The 22,000-square-foot château was completed in 1936. With an imposing masculine facade clad in concrete and granite, it projects a strong presence that protects its elegant and exceptionally crafted interiors.

Upon Anna's death in 1963, Huguette returned to New York and isolated herself in the comfort of her own Fifth Avenue apartment. Later she retired to various hospital rooms—for over twenty years, never returning to Bellosguardo. The house and gardens always remained well maintained, and over the years developed a local air of mystery. The property stands on its own promontory on the coast, next to the bucolic bird sanctuary funded by Anna and Huguette named in honor of Andrée, visible from the highway. Many wondered just what went on in that astonishing house on the hill, but it remained inaccessible to anyone except groundskeepers, even after Huguette's death at 104 in 2011. However, this time capsule, an opulent home frozen in situ, is starting to be opened; a foundation established to honor the Clark legacy and serve as a focal point for art and culture in Santa Barbara maintains the estate today and plans to open it to the public.

Left: An unmatched facade. The formidable approach to an equally elegant interior.

Left: A citrus garden surrounds a pond framed in boxwood with frescoes as a backdrop.

Above: Another friend.

Above and Opposite: The library, with volumes staggered on the shelves, a rare maintenance. The reception room.

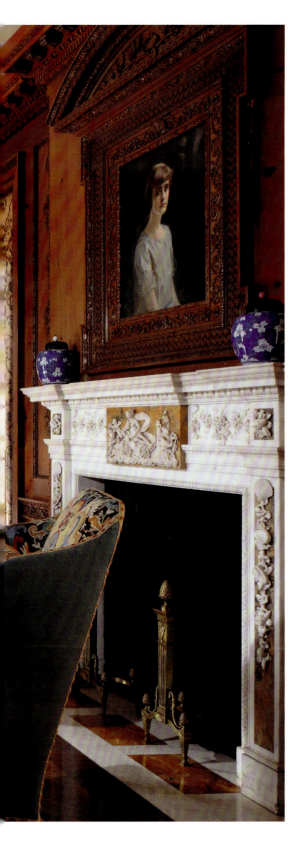

215

Above and Opposite: The dining room, with place cards intact, and the sitting room, both replete with impeccable boiserie.

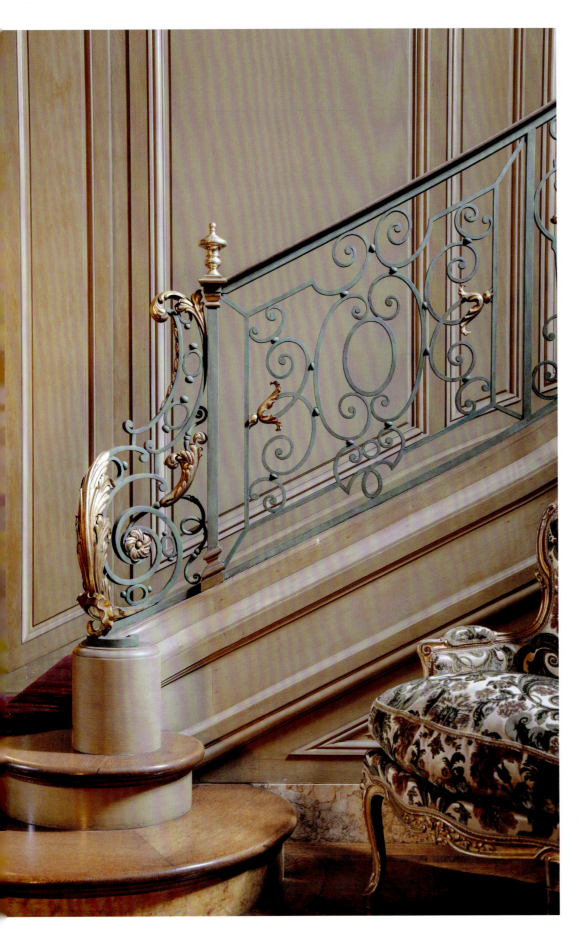

Left: Refined details from ironwork to tooled marble have been carefully maintained at Bellosguardo.

Opposite top: Huguette was an accomplished painter and musician, and her music room has been faithfully preserved.

Opposite bottom: A bath like no other, featuring the original scale and beautifully disguised cabinet doors.

Following Pages: The grand view from the lawn.

CASA BIENVENIDA, DIETERICH ESTATE

Montecito, 1928–1931

Addison Mizner, architect

Lockwood de Forest Jr., rose garden landscape architect

Architect Addison Mizner was a tour de force who left an immense impression on American architecture in the early part of the twentieth century. Mizner, a polymath, proved to be an architectural genius. He led an adventurous life, traveled extensively and distilled his memories into a library of references that informed his eye and hand.

At the end of World War I in 1919, Mizner transformed what was to be his first commission, a hospital for returning soldiers that was no longer needed, into the venerable Everglades Club that would cater to the nation's social elite. His career was quickly propelled by this design, with its towering Mediterranean presence that came to define the Palm Beach look.

Although Mizner is most well-known for the indelible mark that he left on Palm Beach, the house he considered his best work was realized in Montecito. He was given the commission by Union Carbide co-founder Alfred Dieterich in 1928; Mizner knew he was dying and began work immediately. Casa Bienvenida is a grand house with nods to the Medieval and Gothic, yet its floor plan is Palladian, with cloisters on three sides around a courtyard, which allows the sun to find its way into all rooms throughout the day. The main axis runs south to north, anchored by a statue at the far southern end of the great lawn, through the center of the living room, continuing through the courtyard and up the fountained incline to the Mary McLaughlin Craig-designed classical teahouse at the top of the garden. The south entry features a cathedral scale groin-vaulted ceiling, and the living room houses a massive, ancient stone fireplace procured from a castle in the Pyrenees. Mizner designed and manufactured many of the elements of the house, including the Venetian Gothic coral stone window surrounds and other details, as well as the sixty-six exaggerated crawfish fountains, cast in the shops of Mizner Industries, and inspired by the Renaissance garden at Villa Lante in Tuscany.

Noted painter and naturalist Lockwood de Forest Jr. was responsible for planting the rose garden based on Mizner's design. It remains intact today, carefully aligned on axis with the house.

Mizner completed his grand vision in 1931. He considered Casa Bienvenida to be his best house. Dieterich was likely pleased as well. Sadly, neither got to enjoy the fruits of his labor for long, as Mizner passed away in 1933, and, Dieterich in 1935. It may not only be Mizner's greatest work, it could also be the Santa Barbara region's greatest extant golden age estate, as well as one of the finest homes in America.

Left: The imposing facade of the house features references to the great eras of architecture, masterfully woven together.

Right: The courtyard.

Above: The enormous fireplace, procured by Mizner, is purported to be from the Pyrenees and very old. The Fortuny and Schiaparelli pieces are notable examples of modern Italian design.

Center: The remarkable groin-vaulted entry hall.

Above: One of the three remarkable cloisters.

Following Pages: The library.

Above: The living room.

Above: The dining room.

Left: The rose garden, on axis with the view from Ms. Dieterich's bedroom, lovingly well-kempt to this day.

ARCADY PAVILION, KNAPP ESTATE

Montecito, 1905–Today

Carleton Monroe Winslow, Mary McLaughlin Craig, architects

What has become known as the Arcady Pavilion is actually a neo-classical house built atop the sunken music pavilion; that was originally part of a much larger estate since parceled off. In 1911, industrialist and Union Carbine co-founder George Owen Knapp purchased seventy acres of land on this splendid hilltop in Montecito and began the development of a storied estate that grew to some two hundred acres; it was later subdivided. As different configurations of follies, pools, and structures came and went, the core landscape around the pavilion, designed by Carleton Monroe Winslow, remains relatively intact with the exception of the remarkable restoration and additions done by the current owners.

Looking north from the great lawn, the music pavilion was positioned so that its idyllic backdrop of the Santa Ynez Mountains framed by Australian eucalyptus became a ubiquitous image of the Eden that was this place. In 1954 architect Mary McLaughlin Craig was tasked with adding the one-story house atop the existing structure. Subsequent owners worked with *antiquaire* Craig Wright and architect Jack Warner to rework the house to reflect an austere modern response to a Greco-Roman form. Today it has been further refined and stands at the center of a revitalized and reimagined set of interconnecting outdoor spaces set on the original axis put in place over one hundred years ago. The garden's structure still anchors the setting, and despite all the changes, continues to retain its gracious and idyllic pose.

Right: The entrance gate to the main lawn.

Following Pages: The stately Arcady Pavilion today.

Above: The new pool.

Opposite: Elements old and new adorn the gardens.

Above and Right: Original statuary, grottos, and other garden ornaments decorate the landscape.

Left: Old oaks surround a garden on this ever-changing slope of paradise.

VILLA CORBEAU

Montecito, 2006

Appleton & Associates, architects

Villa Corbeau was built in 2002 and designed by the architect Marc Appleton for himself and his family, drawing inspiration from northern Italian and southern French farmhouses. The tongue-in-cheek name of the estate is a combination of Italian (Villa) and French (Corbeau) in honor of the resident crows of the neighborhood.

Appleton has said he "tried to make it look like an architect had nothing to do with it," that the house would appear to have been "of its place" for a long time—part of Santa Barbara's local Mediterranean vernacular heritage.

The light color coated exterior plaster of the building has a subtle mottled effect, set off by custom-stained mahogany windows and doors made in Italy, and salvaged clay roof tiles from Spain. On the interior, the house was similarly provincial in style, with distressed Italian limestone and French oak plank floors, antique beamed ceilings, and mottled plaster walls. The steps from the gravel motor court to the rustic oak plank front door were made from leftover antique limestone pieces Appleton had collected over the years from his other projects.

The overall property plan is a complex of several buildings, reinforcing the farmhouse association. The original garden, which Appleton also planned, was designed to look like a Mediterranean garden gone to seed. It was laid out with vistas and pathways connecting various destinations and outbuildings. Most of the pathways were decomposed granite with steps of local Santa Barbara sandstone.

The axial geometry of the garden layout lends a kind of order to the whole, but the vegetation was left to overgrow its borders, intruding here and there, crowding the pathways, and creating a slightly unkempt, older-looking landscape, an effect which became apparent within just a few years after the garden was planted. Part of the garden was devoted to agricultural produce, with a walled kitchen garden, an orchard of stone-fruit and citrus trees, a potting bench, a henhouse, and a compost area.

Following Appleton's divorce, the property was sold several years ago to new owners, who have made the house their own, adding to and significantly expanding the garden, all the while honoring the original vision and architectural premise of the romantic country farmhouse. They reached out to Appleton and continued to engage his services, turning what was initially a sad transition for him into a joyful collaboration and close friendship.

Left: The walled entry court is surrounded by oaks and native shrubs and features a Tipuana tipu tree in the center.

Following Pages: The kitchen. The living room/library is formally wood paneled and painted French gray with gold leaf details.

Above: An antique French fireplace occupies a corner of the dining room, which looks out on three sides of the garden.

Right: Another view of the dining room.

Left: All one needs to write.

Opposite: A giant bird-of-paradise shades an antique stone fountain and the path leading to more gardens beyond.

Left: A quintessential Southern California outdoor room, shaded by native oak trees.

Above: Heirloom friends in the garden.

Opposite: The fountain celebrates the crossroads of the garden paths with the pool house beyond.

ACKNOWLEDGMENTS

Allegra, thank you for all of your encouragement and support. None of this would have been possible without you. Christopher and Lauren, I am grateful for you both. You are all inspirations.

Matt Walla, your keen eye and patience led to countless moments of perfection in this book.

Marc Appleton and Brian Tichenor, it is an honor to share pages with you. Thank you so much for enriching this volume.

Cristi Walden, always showing up along the path. Thanks again.

Thank you to all of the homeowners for opening their doors to us, and to the friends and colleagues who helped connect the threads along the way. We really appreciate your enthusiasm so much.

With gratitude to:

Scott and Ashley Adelson
Rebecca Anderson
Allie Baxter
Kathleen Brewster
Anne Carty
Edward Carty
Jeff and Satie Chemnick
Rick Closson
Brad and Cheryl Cohen
Glynne and Gillian Couvillion
William Curran and Mara Hochman
Mario Dacunha
Greg Dahlen and Christi Walden
Bruce and Jane Defnet
Eric Goode
Larry and Sharon Grassini
Stephen Harby and Kritsada
    Buajudhavudhivudh
Joanna Kerns
Erin Lammers
Jeremy Lindaman
Thomas Lloyd-Butler and Dan Zelen
Jeremy McBride
Crysta Metzger
Eric Naglemann
Erik Nickel and Michael Loftis
Alexis Plank
Lorie Porter
Richard Ross and Maury Treman
George Schoellkopf and
    Gerald Incandela
Claudia Schou
The Shafer and Lloyd-Butler Families
Jon and Pam Shields
Raun Thorp
Bobby Webb and Michael Corbett
Barbara K. Woods

A huge thank you to Charles Miers for your continued trust and support and to Douglas Curran for your astute guidance and admirable patience over the years. We are grateful to you both. Lastly, to Gisela Aguilar, thank you for seeing it through.
DWW

Above: Santa Barbara from Casa de Leon.